EDGE BOOKS™

DOGS ON THE JOB

THERAPY DOGS

by Walter Roberts, Jr.

Consultant:
Ilene Cohen-Pearson
President
Therapy Pets of the Red River Valley

CAPSTONE PRESS
a capstone imprint

Edge Books are published by Capstone Press,
1710 Roe Crest Drive, North Mankato, Minnesota 56003
www.capstonepub.com

Library of Congress Cataloging-in-Publication Data
Roberts, Walter, Jr., 1956-
Therapy dogs / by Walter Roberts, Jr.
pages cm – (Edge books. Dogs on the job)
Audience: K to Grade 3.
Includes bibliographical references and index.
ISBN 978-1-4765-0132-1 (library binding)
ISBN 978-1-4765-3388-9 (ebook PDF)
1. Dogs—Therapeutic use—Juvenile literature. 2. Working dogs—Juvenile literature.
I. Title.
RM931.D63R63 2014
636.7088—dc23   2013016189

Editorial Credits
Brenda Haugen, editor; Kyle Grenz, designer; Marcie Spence, media researcher;
Laura Manthe, production specialist

Photo Credits
Alamy Images: David Grossman, 5, Marmaduke St. John, 19, MC Images, 21, ZUMA
Press, 6, 9, 15, 20, 22; Capstone Studio: Karon Dubke, 10, 11, 12, 26, 27, 29; Corbis:
Voktor Korotayev/Reuters, cover; Getty Images: Franck Crusiaux/Gamma-Rapho, 8;
iStockphoto; chapin31, 25; Newscom: David Tacon, 7 (top), Harry Jackson Jr./MCT,
23, Jacek Bednarczyk/EPA, 18; Shutterstock: Dennis Sabo, 16, ifoto, 4, 14, 24, Maljalen,
13, Mario Lopes, cover (rocks), Micimakin, 7 (bottom), Sue McDonald, 17

**The author thanks Judy Simonsen and Bentley, all the Caring Canines,
Murphy and Prairie, and Laurie Roberts for providing information and
ideas for this book.**

Printed in the United States of America in Stevens Point, Wisconsin.
032013   007227WZF13

Table of Contents

CHAPTER 1

A Comforting Presence

Murphy, a golden retriever, spends his days bringing comfort to people of all ages. He seems to enjoy working with people, but his life was not always so happy. When Murphy was younger, he was beaten. He was found wandering around in Kentucky, but a rescue group saved him. After he was rescued, Murphy was adopted by a family that gave him the care and love he needed. Now Murphy gives back through his work as a therapy dog.

Golden retrievers often make good therapy dogs.

therapy—a treatment for an illness, an injury, or a disability

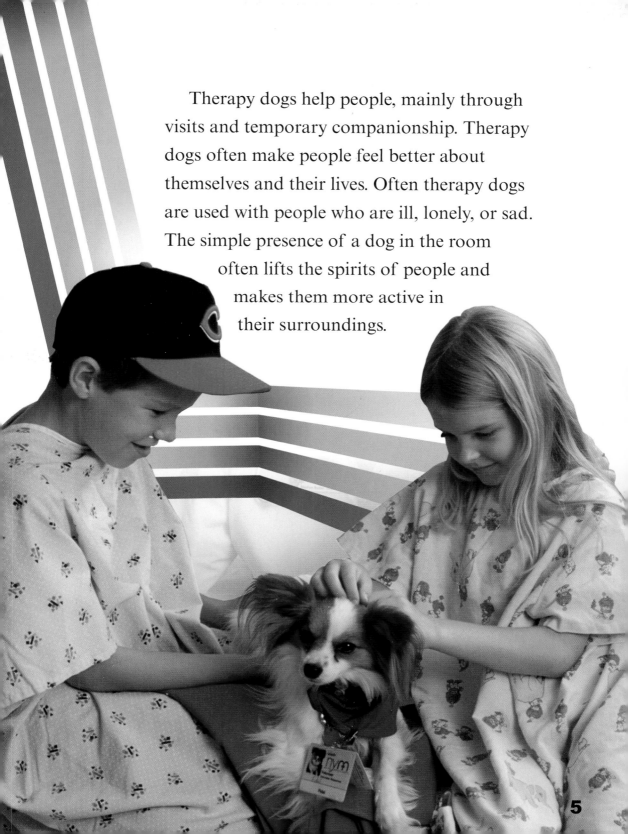

Therapy dogs help people, mainly through visits and temporary companionship. Therapy dogs often make people feel better about themselves and their lives. Often therapy dogs are used with people who are ill, lonely, or sad. The simple presence of a dog in the room often lifts the spirits of people and makes them more active in their surroundings.

Therapy dogs serve in places that ordinary dogs cannot. Therapy dogs work in schools, hospitals, nursing homes, and prisons. Therapy dogs sometimes wear colorful vests with patches identifying them by the work they do.

The vests show people that the dog has special skills and is not just an ordinary dog. Therapy dogs may also wear unique tags to show people that they have special skills. The tags often have the dogs' pictures on them.

FACT

Some therapy dogs wear special bandanas around their necks instead of vests.

Service Dogs

Therapy dogs are often confused with service dogs. Service dogs are more highly trained in specific tasks than therapy dogs are. Service dogs work with people who have special needs. People depend on these animals to help them with their daily needs. These dogs include guide dogs and mobility dogs. Guide dogs help people who are blind. Mobility dogs assist those who are in wheelchairs or have other difficulties moving around. Service dogs can go more places than therapy dogs can. Service dogs are allowed almost everywhere, including restaurants.

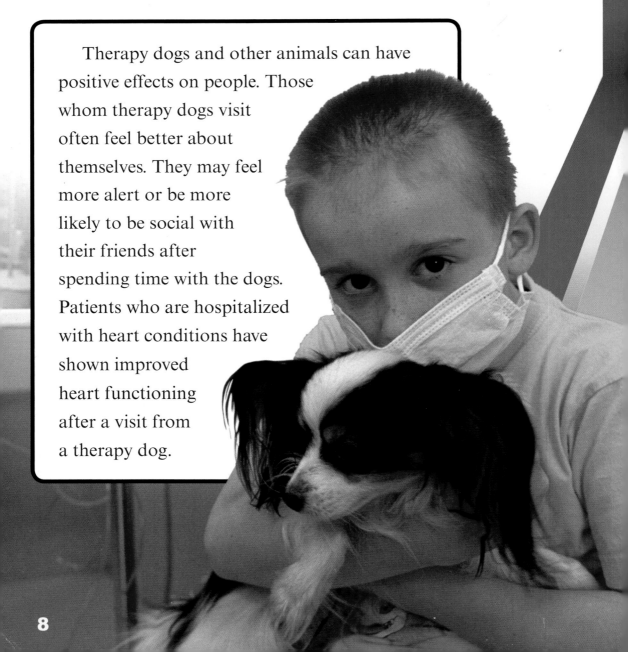

Therapy dogs and other animals can have positive effects on people. Those whom therapy dogs visit often feel better about themselves. They may feel more alert or be more likely to be social with their friends after spending time with the dogs. Patients who are hospitalized with heart conditions have shown improved heart functioning after a visit from a therapy dog.

And it's not only those who are supposed to receive therapy that benefit from a therapy dog's visit. When dogs visit, some staff members say the animals reduce stress for them too.

Helping Soldiers

One of the first therapy dogs was a Yorkshire terrier named Smoky. She was a stray dog found by an American soldier in New Guinea during World War II (1939–1945). Smoky brought happiness to troops she visited. She flew along with soldiers in combat missions and was awarded battle stars for her service. She lived to be 14 years old.

CHAPTER 2

Becoming a Team

A dog that is chosen as a therapy dog receives special training and shows special talents. Any breed of dog can be a therapy dog if it has the right temperament, though many are small and medium size dogs. But no animal can be a therapy dog if it cannot pass the tests to qualify.

breed—a certain kind of animal within an animal group

temperament—the combination of an animal's behavior and personality; the way an animal usually acts or responds to a situation shows its temperament

A therapy dog must follow its handler's directions. A dog first learns basic **obedience** commands. It may learn basic obedience from its handler or from a trainer who helps the handler teach the dog. The animal learns to sit, stay, and come to the handler.

Bringing Back Memories

Judy Simonsen has an unusual therapy dog. Bentley is a 100-pound (45-kilogram) bloodhound. Because of their size, few bloodhounds serve as therapy dogs. But people react to Bentley because of his bloodhound traits—his droopy skin, long ears, and large **muzzle**. Because of Bentley's size, people often like to watch him from a distance or just scratch him on the head.

Many elderly people say Bentley reminds them of bloodhounds from old TV shows, such as *The Beverly Hillbillies* and *Hee Haw*. This form of therapy is called reminiscence. It is not unusual for elderly people to remember, or reminisce, with therapy teams about their past experiences with animals.

obedient—able to follow rules and commands
muzzle—an animal's nose, mouth, and jaws

Once a dog understands basic commands, it is watched in test situations required to become a certified therapy dog. Throughout the world, many organizations test potential therapy dogs. These groups include Pet Partners, Therapy Dogs Incorporated, and Therapy Dog International. While the tests vary slightly depending on the group giving the test, they all look for similar things. They all test how well the dog responds to basic commands and how well the dog and handler work together.

The testing groups also look at the calmness of the dog in a variety of settings, such as schools and hospitals. They examine the comfort of the dog in potentially stressful or difficult situations. For example, a therapy dog must not be bothered by the strange size or shape of medical equipment or the noises the equipment makes.

FACT

The first test many therapy dogs pass is the standards test to be a Canine Good Citizen. Passing this test shows that the dog has good manners at home and in the community.

canine—to do with dogs

CHAPTER 3

On the Job

Once the dog and its handler pass the therapy dog test, they become a therapy dog team. A dog may be friendly without its handler, but it can't be a therapy dog by itself. The best therapy dog teams work together as if they can read one another's minds.

Together the handler and the dog move around the area in which they are working. The handler tries to find the best place to work with a person. Sometimes that means getting close— but not too close—to a person in a wheelchair.

It might mean having the dog put its paws on the side of a hospital bed to make it easier for a person to pet the dog. Often the dog must stay calm and in place when a child becomes excited. Whatever the situation, a therapy dog and its handler work together to give the best type of service for the person receiving therapy.

THERAPY DOG

FACT

Many of the places visited by therapy dogs are noisy. Therapy dogs must remain calm around odd noises and people talking loudly.

Therapy dogs help people in two main ways. They can provide animal-assisted activities or animal-assisted therapy.

Animal-assisted activities are usually short, pleasant visits with people. The visits are meant to bring joy to the people who get to meet and greet the dogs. These activities often occur with groups of people in schools, hospitals, and assisted-living homes.

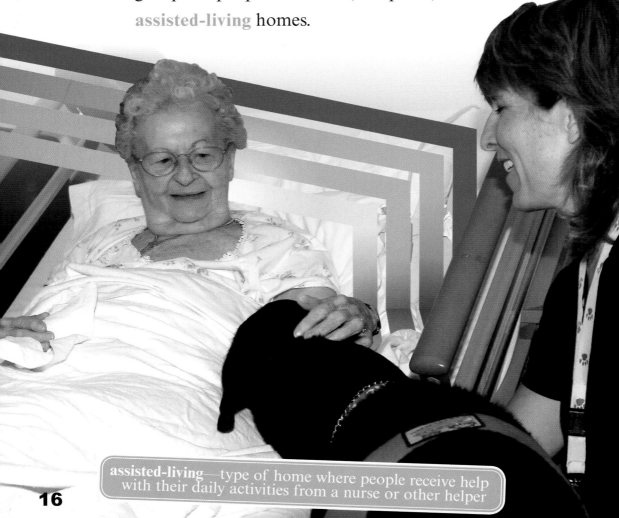

assisted-living—type of home where people receive help with their daily activities from a nurse or other helper

Caring Canines is a group of therapy dog teams who regularly visit places in Minnesota. Caring Canines makes more than 30 visits each year, mostly to assisted-living homes.

All of the therapy dog teams with Caring Canines are volunteers who donate their time to the group. Some of the dogs are purebred, but others are not. Some of the dogs do tricks that delight the people they visit. Other dogs simply have friendly personalities that bring joy to people. Some of the dogs in the group are large. Most of the dogs, however, are medium or small sized, such as shih tzus and Shetland sheepdogs.

Most people feel more comfortable petting small or medium sized dogs.

purebred—having parents of the same breed

Animal-assisted therapy helps people with their problems. Each therapy session is guided by a specialist, such as a professional counselor. The therapy may happen in the same settings as animal-assisted activities but is usually limited to working with one person or small groups.

The therapy usually has a goal. For example, a counselor may have a child work with a dog to help overcome shyness. Or the animal may help a person feel less nervous during a visit to a doctor's office.

Marley, an Australian shepherd, works with children who have difficulty reading. She helps with the READ Program in the Fargo, North Dakota, area. Children practice reading to Marley. The children learn to read better without worrying about being judged or others growing impatient with them.

A therapy dog sits quietly while a child reads a story.

People often think that because therapy dogs are gentle, they can be off of a leash. That is not always true. Therapy dogs must be under the control of their handler at all times. Some dogs follow commands well enough that they can sometimes roam freely within a room.

But handlers usually find it's best to have a leash or **halter** on the dog in case something unexpected happens. Then the handler can quickly remove the therapy dog from the situation if needed.

halter—a strap that fits over an animal's nose and behind its ears that is used to lead the animal

21

The human-animal bond is a strong one. They can become close friends and caretakers. People and animals seem to influence one another in good ways, often unspoken. For example, petting a dog can make a person feel happy. And the dog being petted often reacts with pleasure, which is shown by a wagging tail.

Therapy dogs can teach people how to treat others better, even if the people have been mistreated themselves. Children can learn to show kindness and concern for others by being visited by therapy dogs.

When it is working, a therapy dog is trained to only eat treats from its handler. This prevents the dog from eating things that are unsafe for it, such as medicine that may be on the floor of a hospital.

Sometimes therapy dogs are invited to spend more private time with certain people. A dog may be invited to an elderly person's room or apartment for a longer visit between the dog and the person.

Not for Everyone

Therapy dog handlers must respect the fact that not everyone enjoys dogs—even gentle therapy dogs. In some situations, there may also be rules about who can visit with the dogs. Sometimes a person's culture or medical condition requires that he or she limit contact with dogs. Sometimes people have had bad experiences with dogs in the past. Even seeing a dog may make these people nervous. Handlers are often asked to avoid contact between the animal and the people in these cases.

FACT

A therapy dog must behave politely, not only with visitors, but also with other therapy dogs.

PET ME I'M FRIENDLY

culture—a people's way of life, ideas, customs, and traditions

CHAPTER 4

Off Duty

Therapy dogs spend a great deal of time on the job. But like all dogs, they need time to relax and exercise too. When they are working, therapy dogs have to remain calm, follow rules, and be fairly immobile. When they are not working, it is very important for them to get exercise.

So what do therapy dogs do in their spare time? Run, bark, chase, chew, dig, roll, swim, and sleep—all the things most dogs love to do. As therapy dogs grow older, the stress and excitement of their jobs may become too great. This is a normal part of life for all working animals. Then it's time for the dog to **retire**.

retire—when a person or animal gives up work, usually because of age

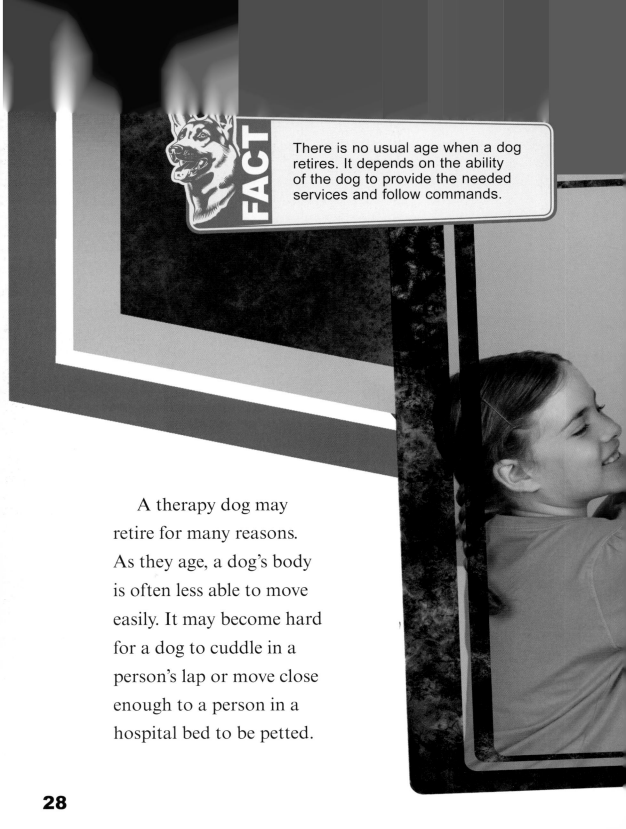

There is no usual age when a dog retires. It depends on the ability of the dog to provide the needed services and follow commands.

A therapy dog may retire for many reasons. As they age, a dog's body is often less able to move easily. It may become hard for a dog to cuddle in a person's lap or move close enough to a person in a hospital bed to be petted.

Most therapy dogs are owned by their handlers. When a dog retires, the partners usually stay together.

Life for the retired therapy dog is one of relaxation. That means more play, more sleep, and more time to spend with the most important people in their lives—their human family.

Glossary

assisted-living (uh-SIST-ed LIH-ving)—type of home where people receive help with their daily activities from a nurse or other helper

breed (BREED)—a certain kind of animal within an animal group

canine (KAY-nyn)—to do with dogs

culture (KUHL-chuhr)—a people's way of life, ideas, customs, and traditions

halter (HAWL-tur)—a strap that fits over an animal's nose and behind its ears that is used to lead the animal

muzzle (MUHZ-uhl)—an animal's nose, mouth, and jaws

obedient (oh-BEE-dee-uhnt)—able to follow rules and commands

purebred (PYOOR-bred)—having parents of the same breed

retire (ri-TIRE)—when a person or animal gives up work, usually because of age

temperament (TEM-pur-uh-muhnt)—the combination of an animal's behavior and personality; the way an animal usually acts or responds to a situation shows its temperament

therapy (THER-uh-pee)—a treatment for an illness, an injury, or a disability

trait (TRATE)—a quality or characteristic that makes one animal different from another

Read More

Baines, Becky. *Everything Dogs: All the Canine Facts, Photos, and Fun You Can Get Your Paws On!* Everything. Washington, D.C.: National Geographic Children's Books, 2012.

Bozzo, Linda. *Therapy Dog Heroes.* Amazing Working Dogs. Berkeley Heights, N.J.: Bailey Books/Enslow, 2011.

Larrew, Brekka Hervey. *Golden Retrievers.* All about Dogs. Mankato, Minn.: Capstone Press, 2009.

Internet Sites

FactHound offers a safe, fun way to find Internet sites related to this book. All of the sites on FactHound have been researched by our staff.

Here's all you do:

Visit *www.facthound.com*

Type in this code: 9781476501321

Check out projects, games and lots more at
www.capstonekids.com

Index